This Messy Entertainment book belongs to:

....

....

Dawn the Dolphin

Published By Messy Entertainment Ltd 2017
ISBN 978-1-9998015-4-0
Messy Entertainment Ltd
www.messyentertainment.com

Dawn The Dolphin 2017 © Messy Entertainment Ltd
All rights reserved.

This book or any portion thereof may not be reproduced or used
in any manner whatsoever without the express written permission
of the publisher except for the use of brief quotations in a book review.

One day when the sea was calm and the sun was high in the sky, a pod of young dolphins were playing tag in the perfectly blue sea.

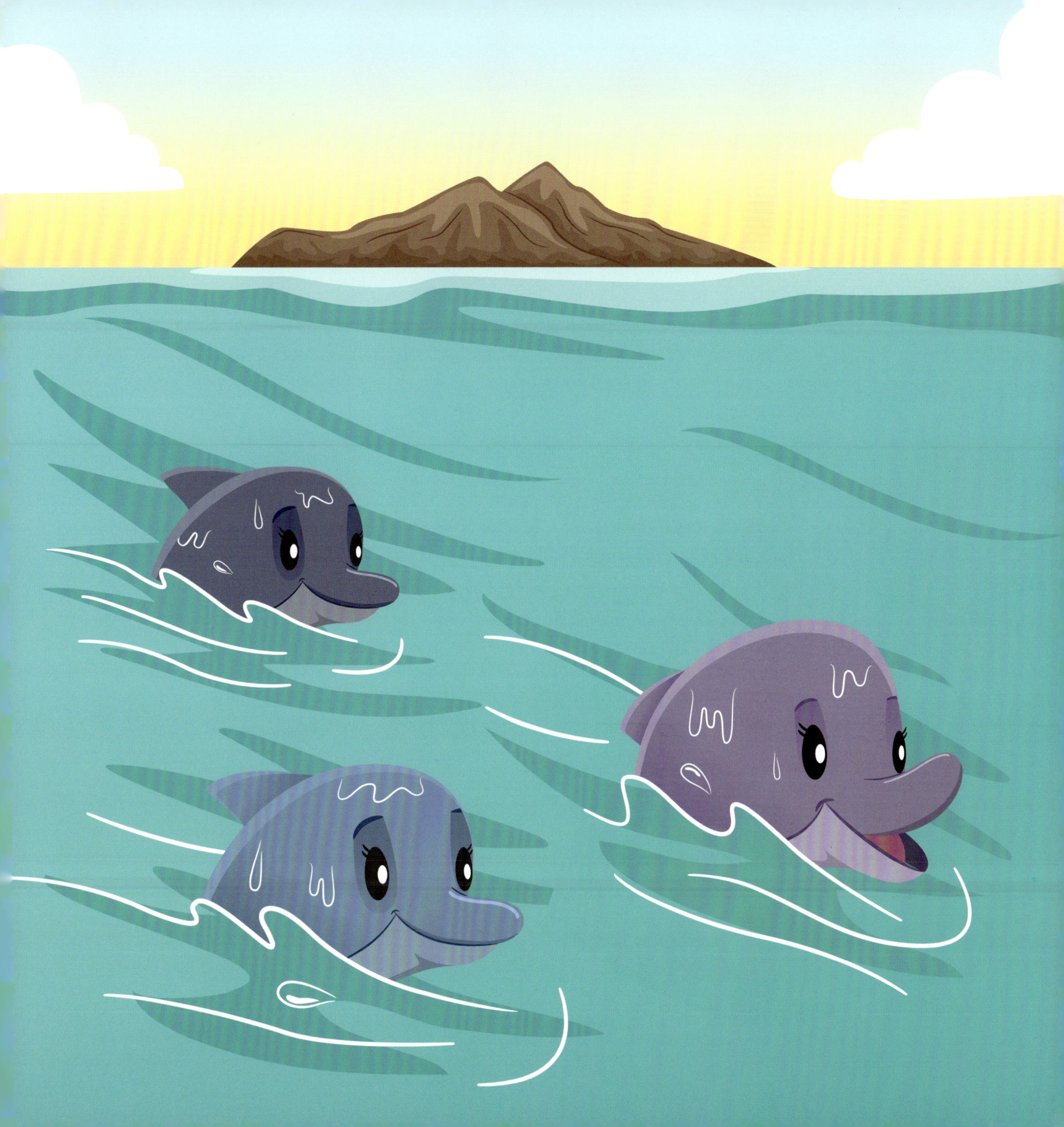

"Dawn wait for us!" shouted her friends, Tessa, Gypsie and Rosie, as they chase her all the way down to the bottom of the sea.

Dawn is the smallest dolphin and the best at swimming so the other dolphins struggle to catch her.

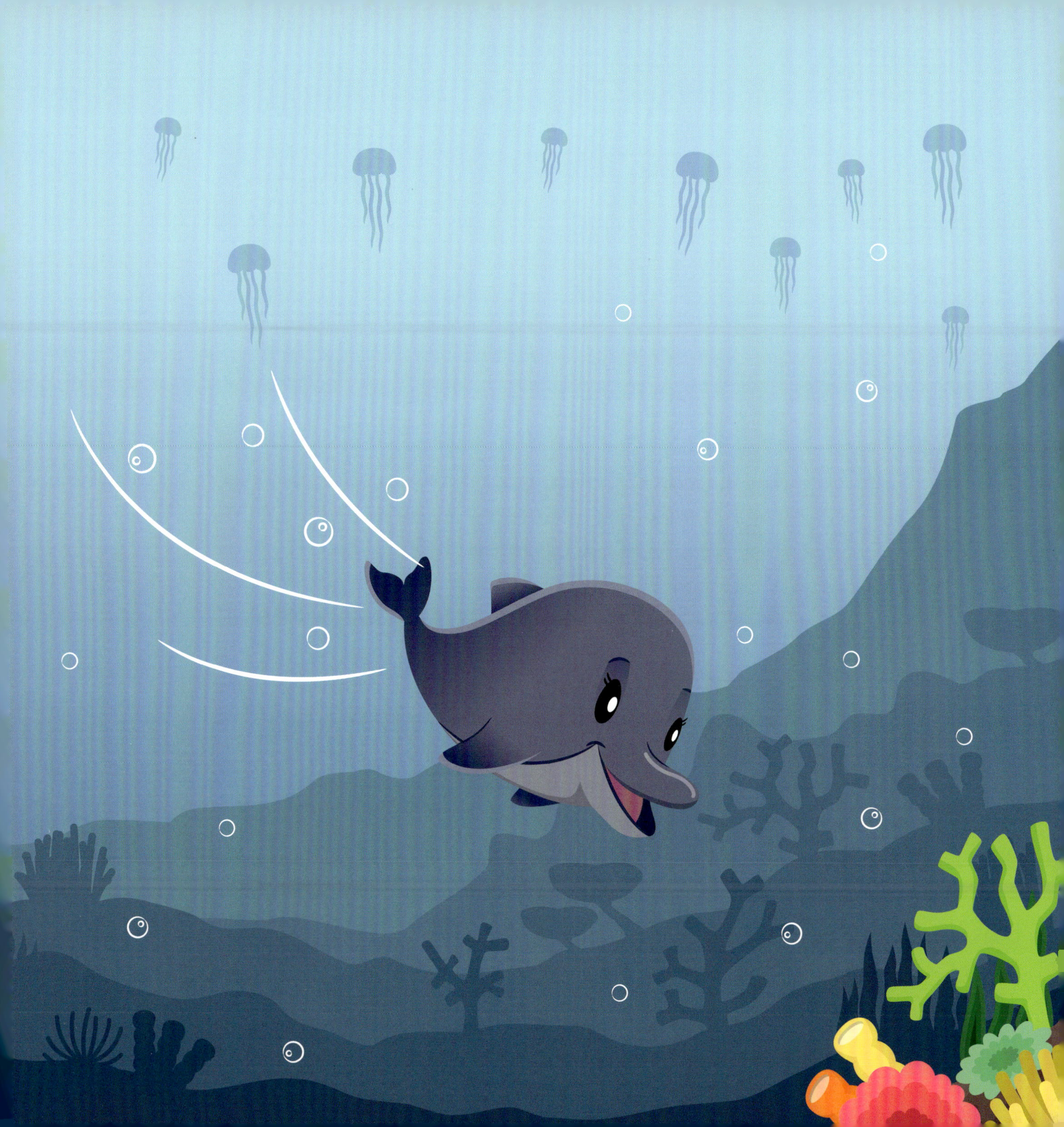

Dawn swims in and out of the boat wreck but her friends are no longer behind her, "I think they've given up chasing me".

"This is boring, lets go and eat" says Rosie.

As they turn around in search of fish for dinner, Rosie says "Tessa knows where the best fish swim, she's going to show us so we can catch some for our dinner".

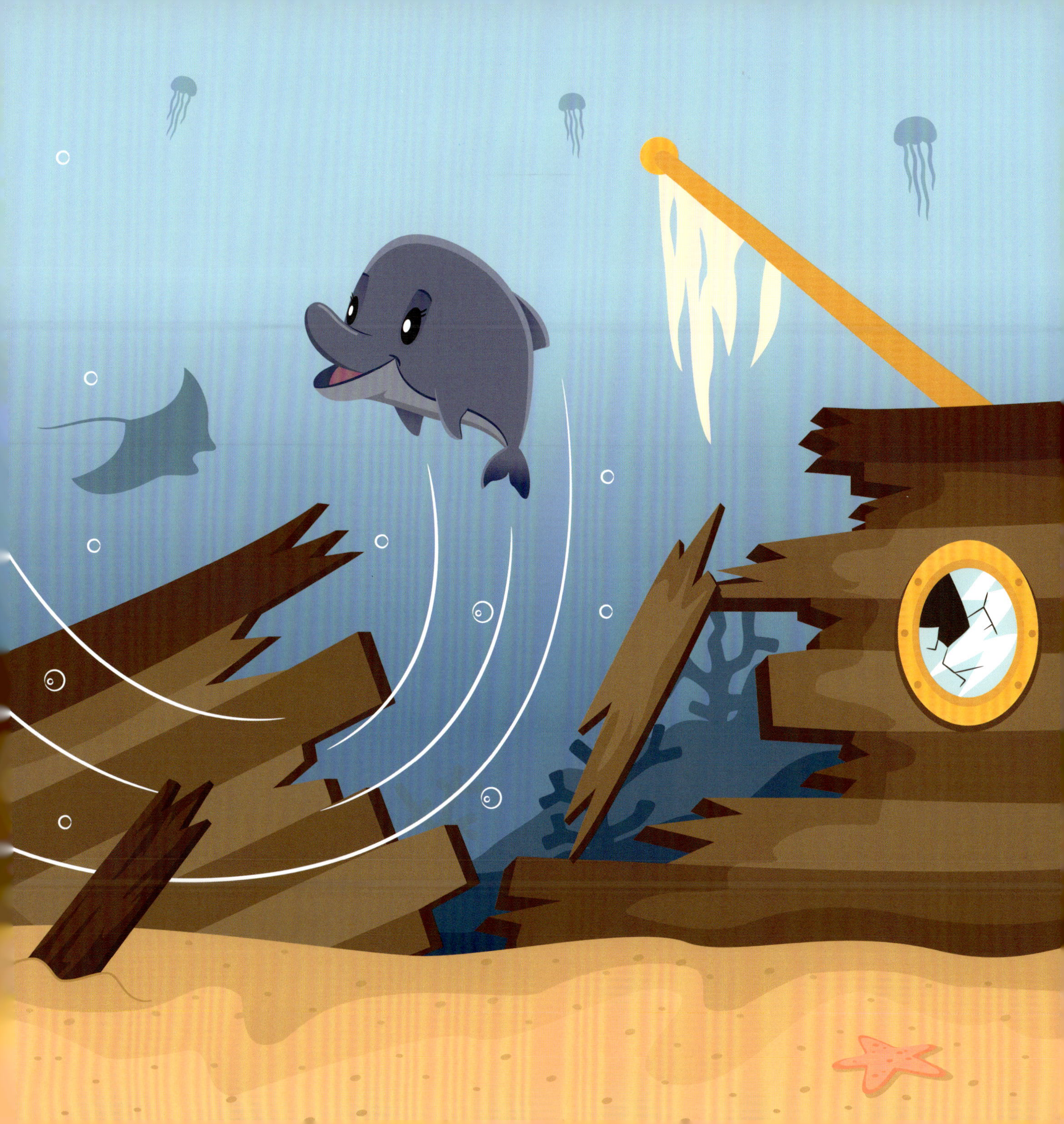

"Lets go to the harbour again, there was lots of fish there last time" shouts Gypsie.

"Follow me" says Tessa. Tessa always goes to the harbour for fish.

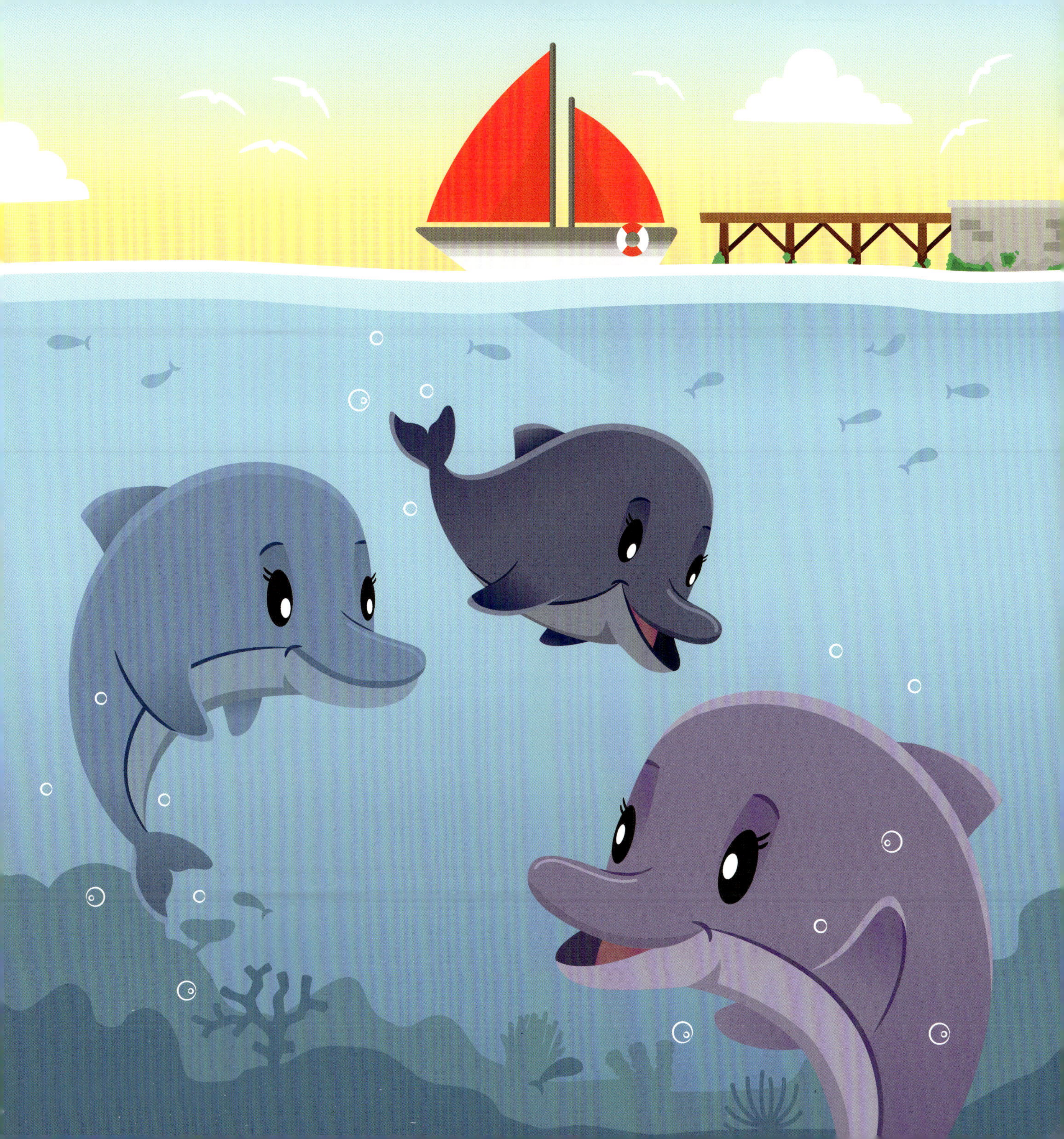

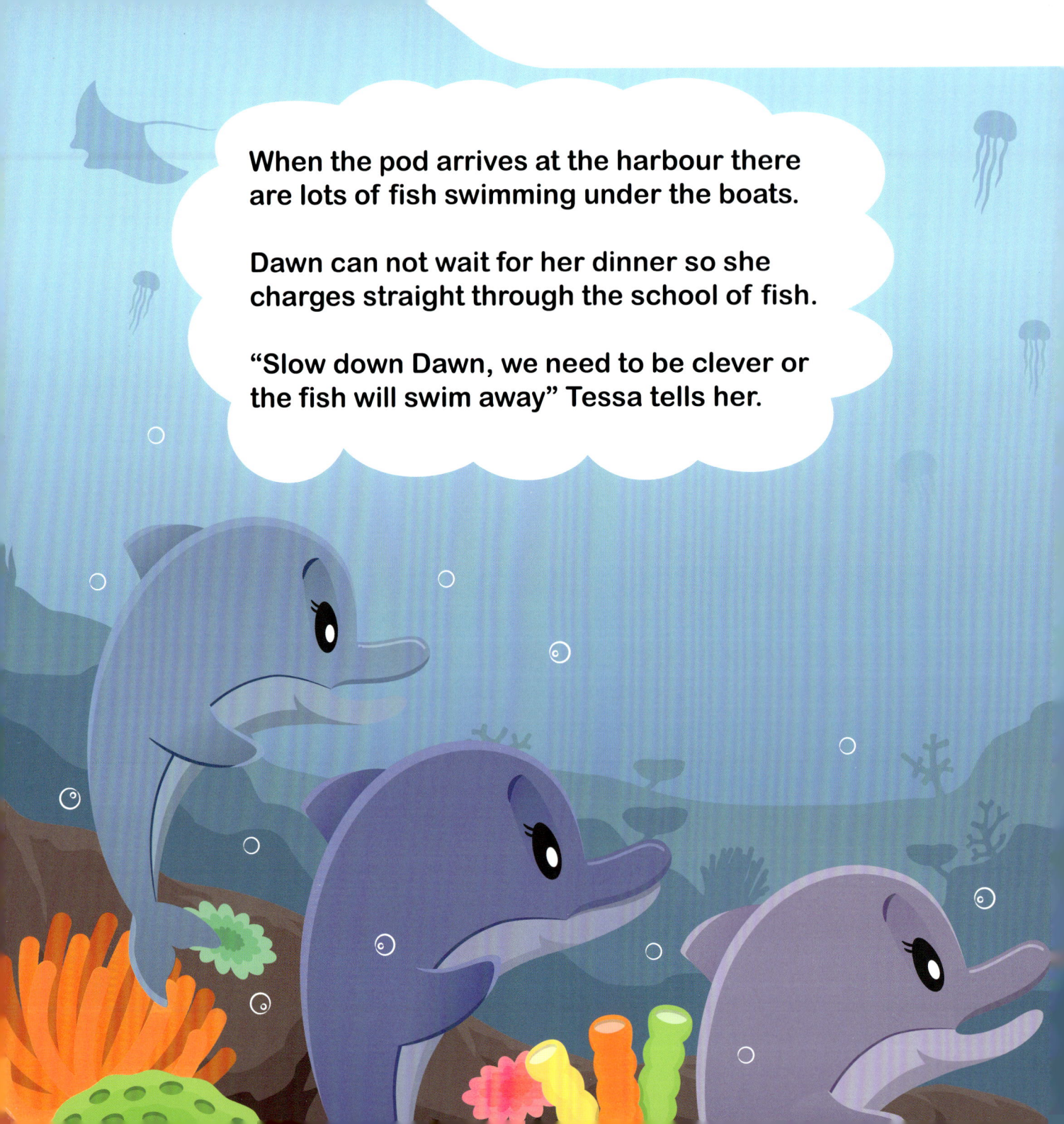

When the pod arrives at the harbour there are lots of fish swimming under the boats.

Dawn can not wait for her dinner so she charges straight through the school of fish.

"Slow down Dawn, we need to be clever or the fish will swim away" Tessa tells her.

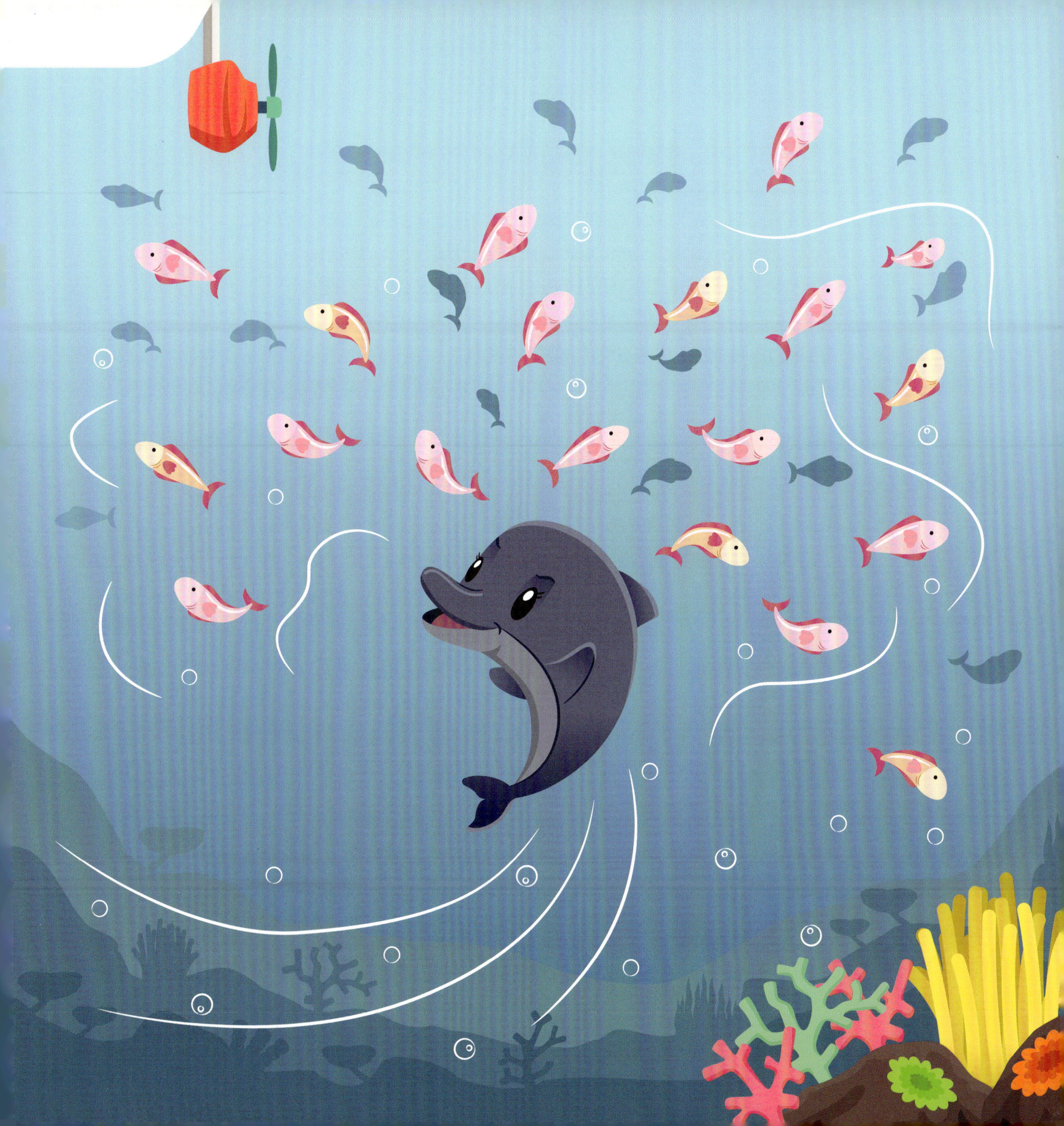

"Come on, lets practice our technique" says Gypsie.

All three dolphins circle the fish to make them cluster together, then one at a turn the dolphins shoot through the school taking a big mouthful of fish.

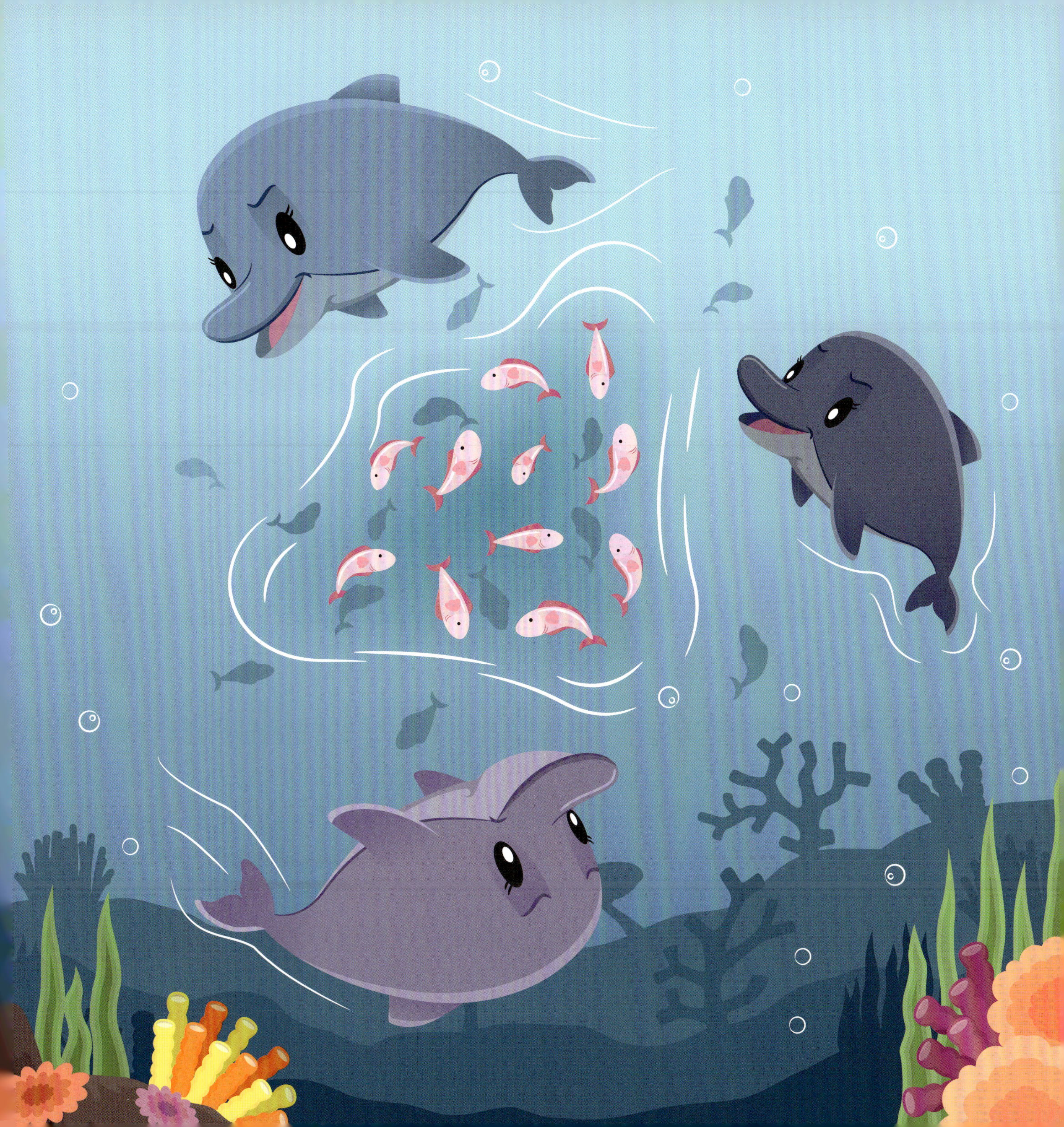

As Dawn, Gypsie and Rosie are busy eating, Tessa swims towards a boat that is floating a short distance away.

Humans are in the water but Tessa seems to think that something is wrong so she has to investigate.

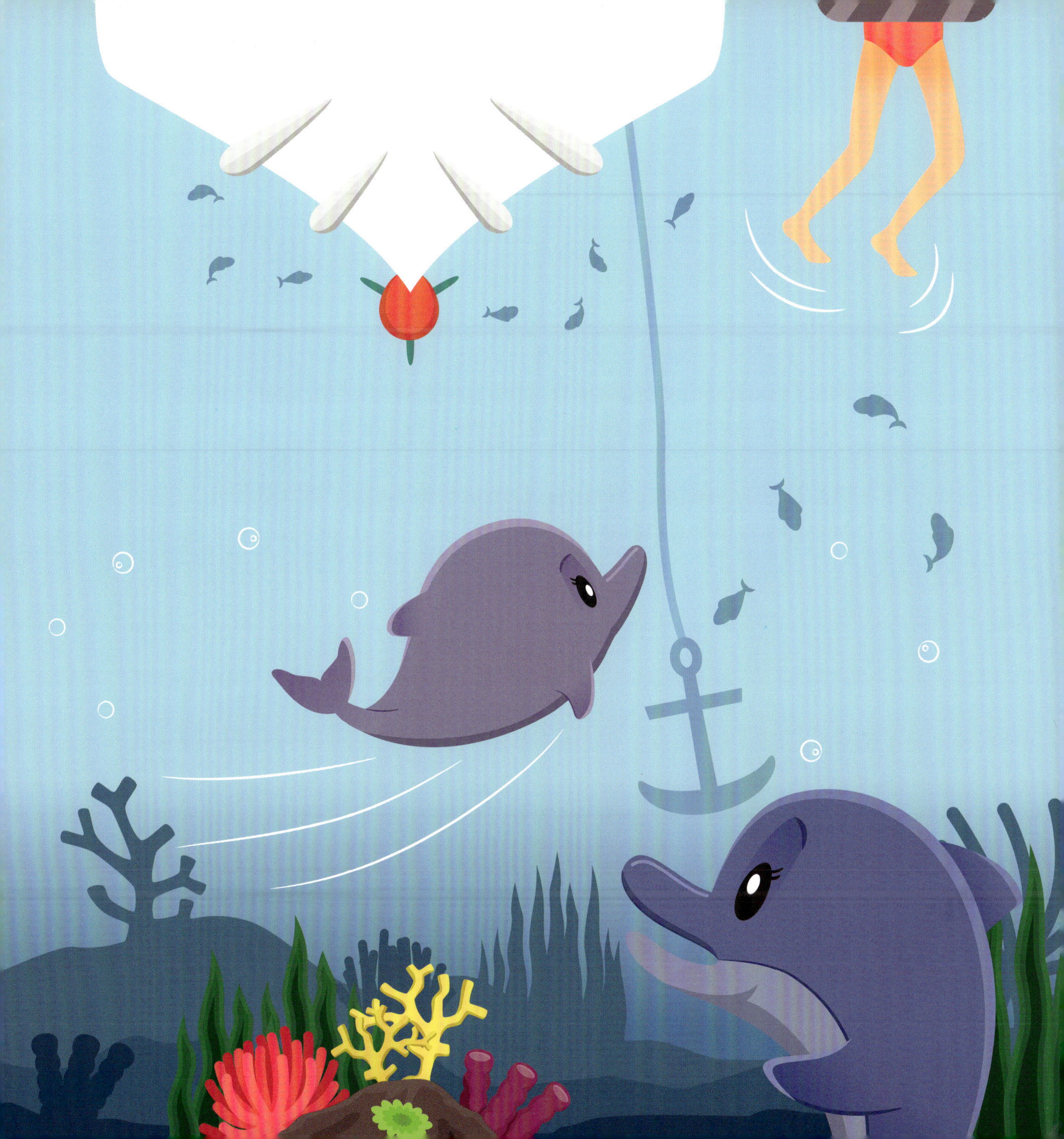

As Tessa gets closer to the boat she can see that Grey the shark is patrolling near by.

As Tessa swims over to Grey she asks "What are you doing here Grey?".

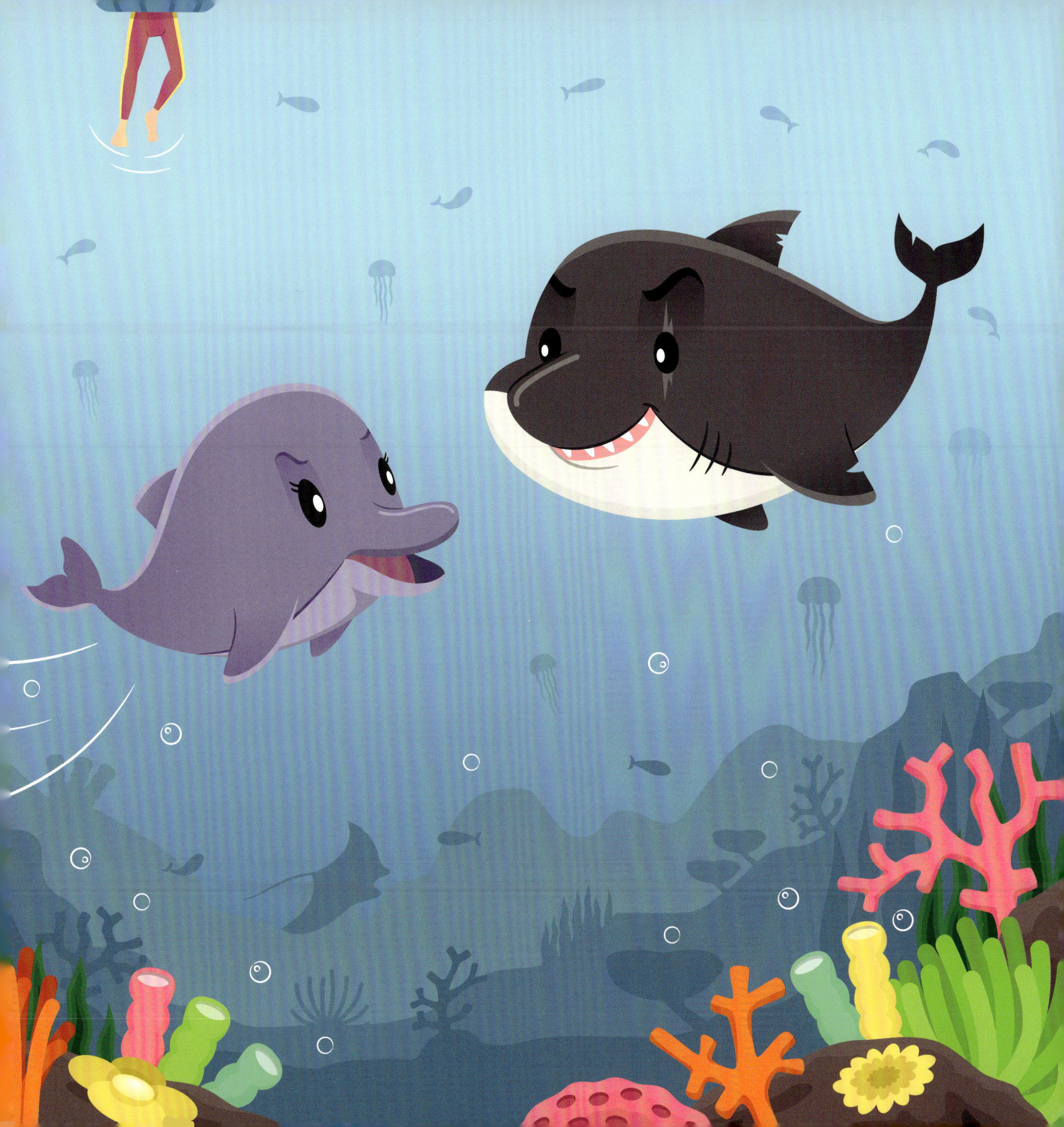

"Hello Tessa, fancy seeing you here, you know I like to check out the area for a tasty supper" Grey says mischievously.

"Well I want you to go home Grey, this is no place for a shark, I don't like you being this close to the humans" replies Tessa.

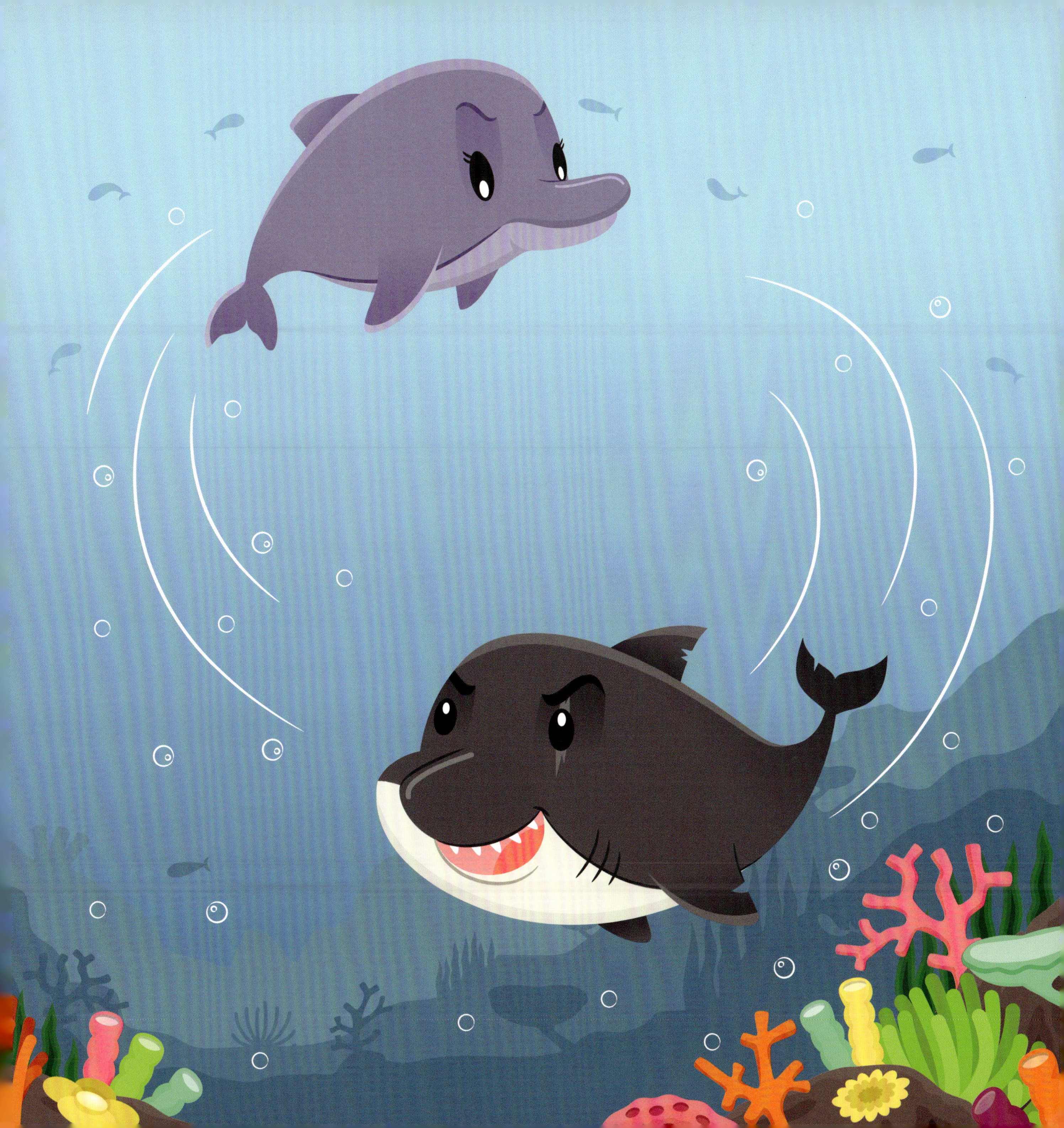

"I have changed, I don't bite humans now, you wouldn't mind if I were to stay would you Tessa?" Grey suggests.

"You heard her Grey" says Dawn as she swims really fast around Grey with great confidence.

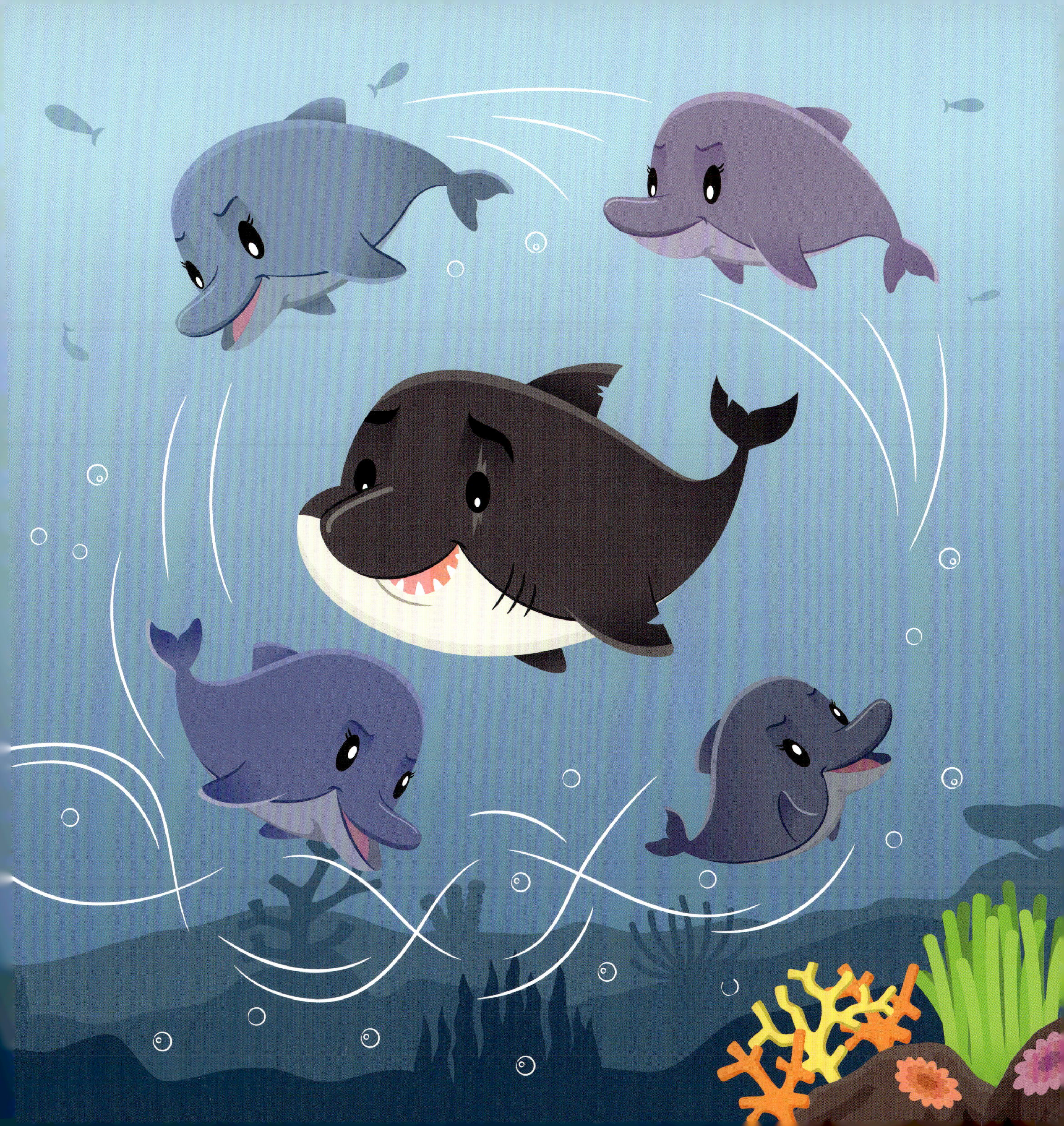

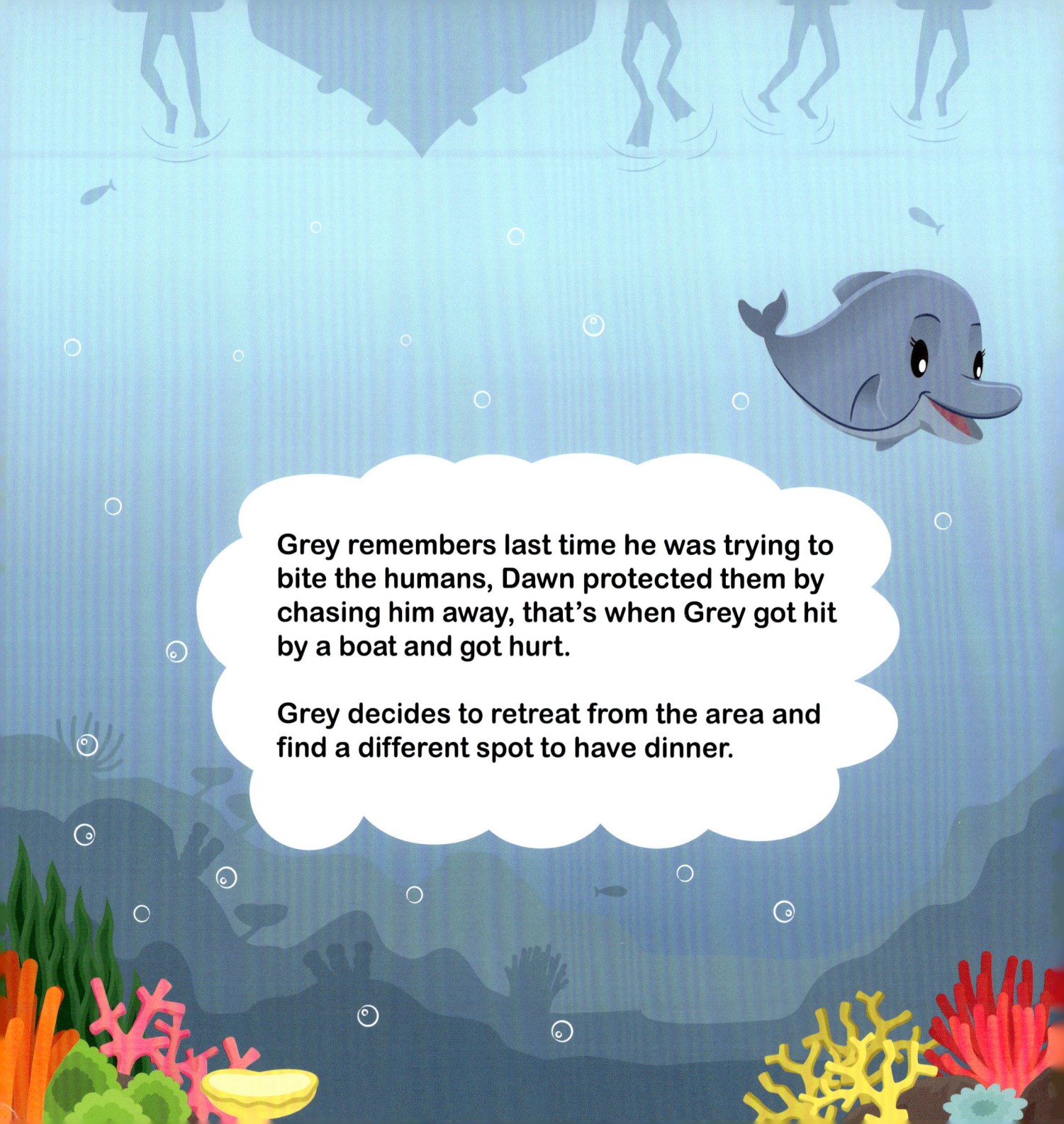

Grey remembers last time he was trying to bite the humans, Dawn protected them by chasing him away, that's when Grey got hit by a boat and got hurt.

Grey decides to retreat from the area and find a different spot to have dinner.

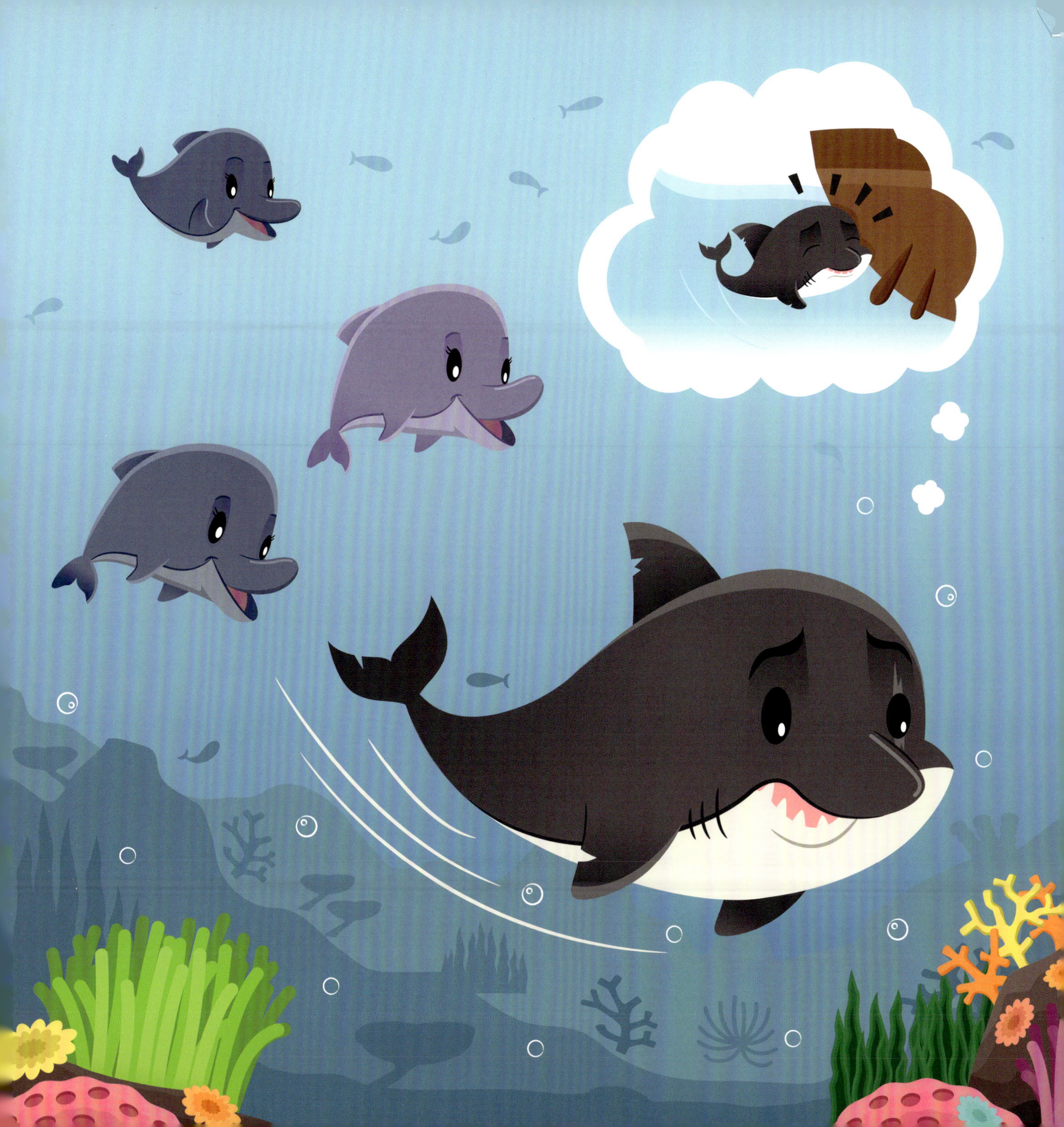

"Dawn you were amazing" says Rosie.

"I think we are all amazing for keeping the humans safe, now lets do some jumps and show off in front of them, who's in?" says Dawn excitedly.

The people watch in amazement as the young pod show off their jumping skills under the moon light.

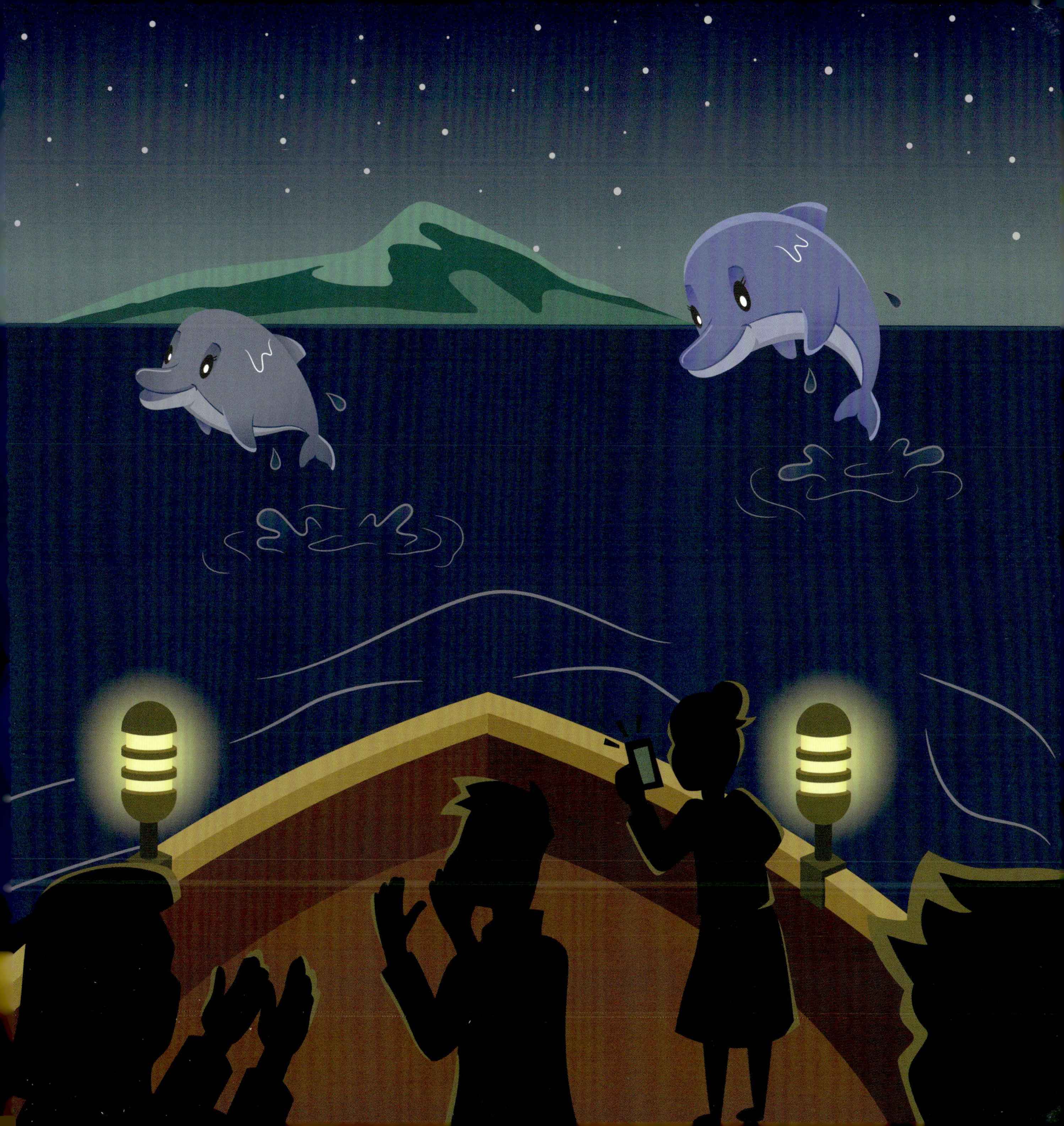

ALL ABOUT ME...

Dolphin

- We can grow to be 2-4 metres in length
- We can swim over 30 kilometres per hour
- We use echo location to hunt and navigate
- We can dive as deep as 250 metres
- We are carnivores and eat mostly fish

We live in every ocean of the world except the Arctic and the Antarctic oceans

Conservation Status

- Critically Endangered
- Endangered
- Vulnerable
- Near Threatened
- *Least Concerned*

Bottlenose Dolphins are not considered to be an endangered species in 2017.

Bottlenose Dolphin

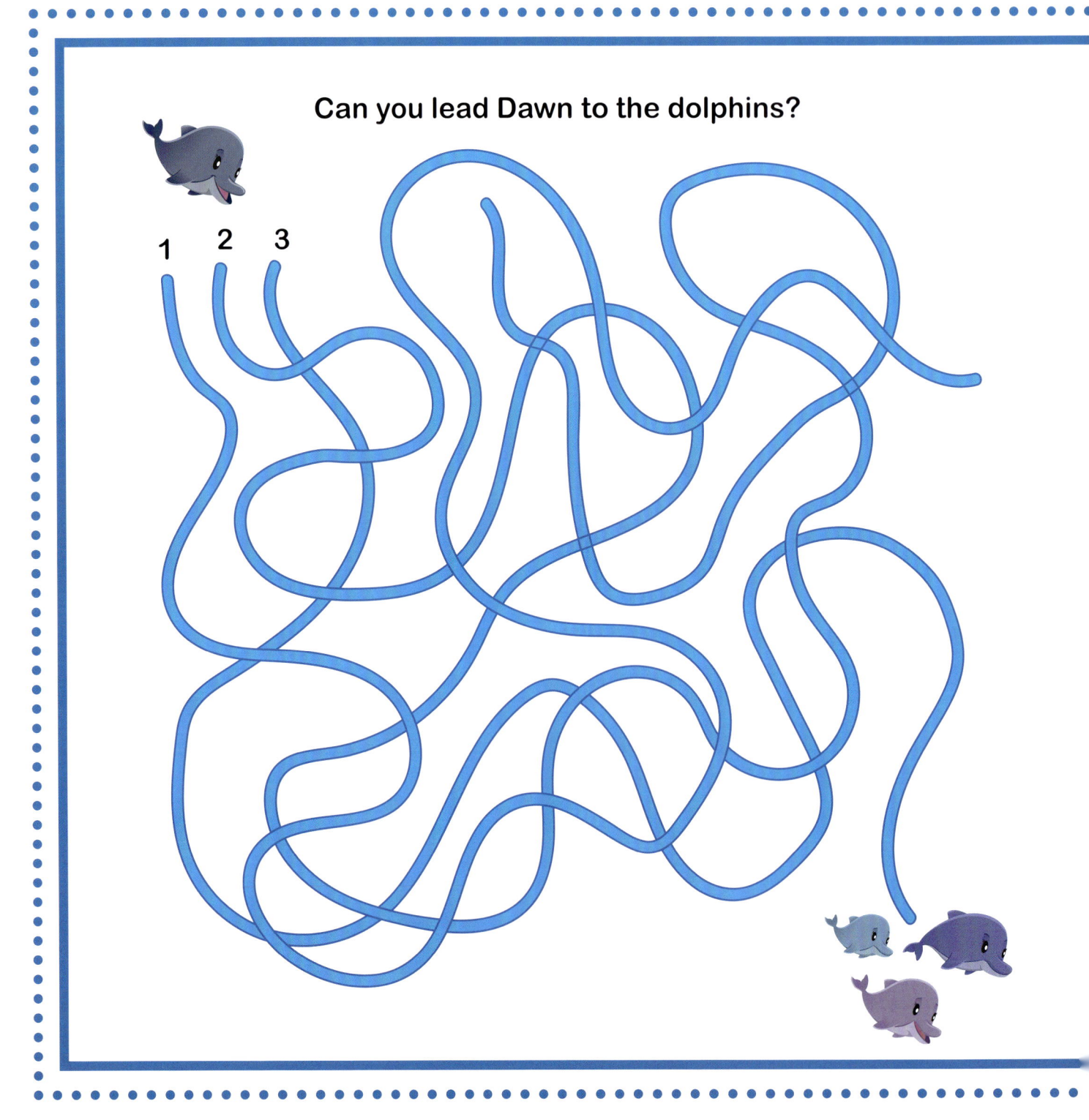

Can you lead Dawn to the dolphins?

1 2 3

Can you add together these dolphins?

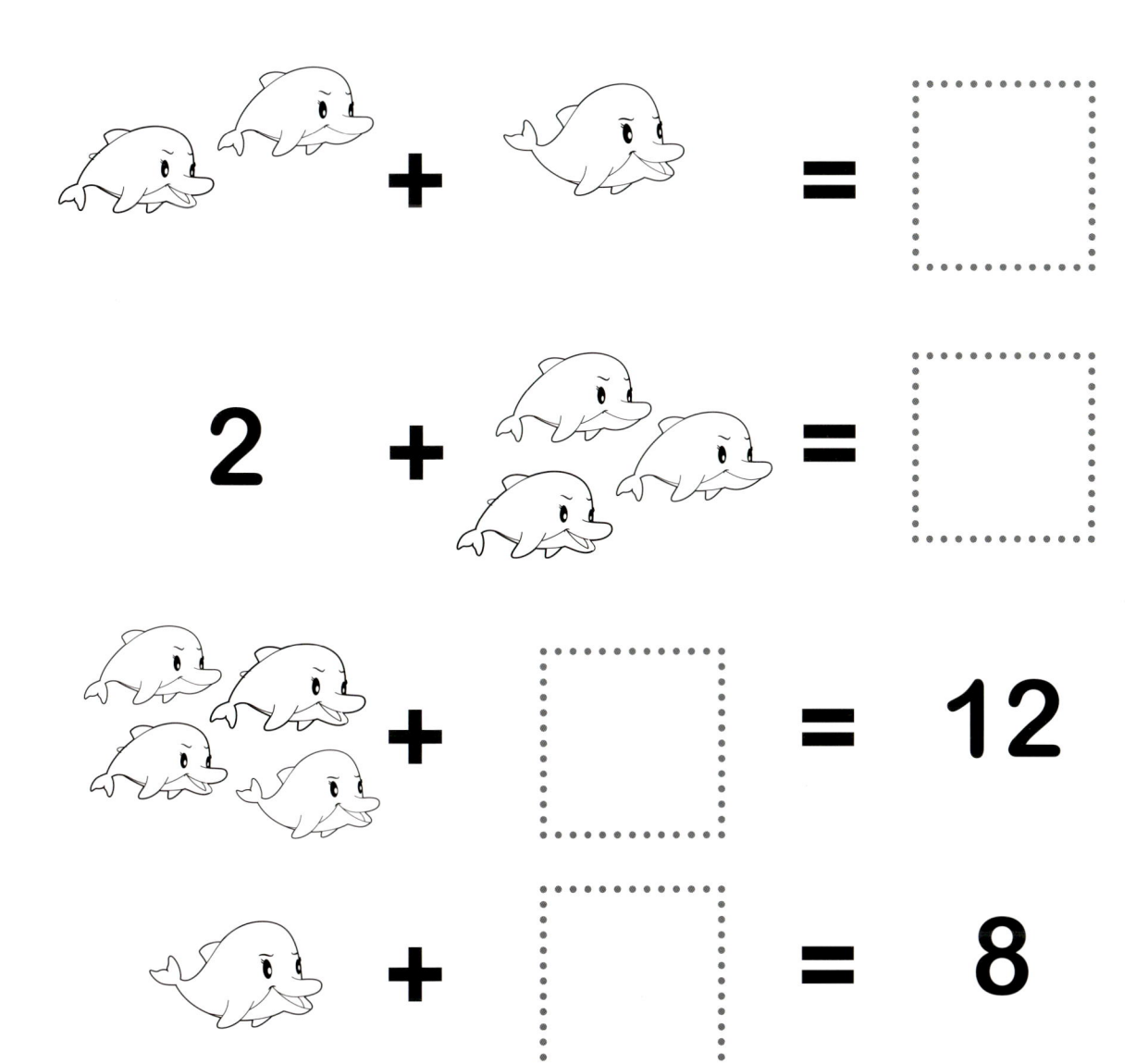

Can you find 7 differences?

Can you find the way through the maze?

Can you find these words?

| DOLPHIN | SWIM | ECHO | JUMP |
| SPLASH | FRIENDS | POD | BOAT |

F	G	H	E	B	O	A	T
S	W	R	C	T	Y	S	U
P	D	B	H	J	R	D	H
L	P	S	O	U	A	N	R
A	O	Q	W	M	V	E	B
S	D	O	L	P	H	I	N
H	M	V	X	D	E	R	A
T	M	S	W	I	M	F	O
P	L	K	E	R	S	Y	C

Can you fill in the missing letters?

echo

dolphin

ocean

jump

○ ○ h ○

　　　 l

○ u ○ ○

　　　 ○

　　　 ○

○ c ○ ○ n

OCEAN SERIES

www.messyentertainment.com

Search 'Messy Entertainment'
for books, apps & much more.